WHAT'S
LOVE
GOT TO DO WITH IT?

THE CASE FOR
SAME SEX MARRIAGE

Senators
RAYMOND J. LESNIAK
LORETTA WEINBERG

ACKNOWLEDGMENTS

Senators

RAYMOND J. LESNIAK

LORETTA WEINBERG

Thanks go first and foremost to the thousands of members of Garden State Equality, LGBT and straight, young and old, male and female, from every religious tradition or none, who circulated petitions, called and e-mailed their legislators, prayed and protested, with one common goal — EQUALITY.

To Kean University, in keeping with its commitment to human rights, and in particular President Dawood Farahi, Audrey Kelly and Joey Moran. Thank you for putting the words, the images, the ideas and the principles on these pages.

To Felice Vazquez, whose idea it was to publish this book; 20th Legislative District Chief of Staff Erin Caragher and legislative aides Amy Naples and John Vazquez; and, New Jersey Civil Rights Commissioner Salena Carroll — you contributed to this effort every step of the way.

To Senator Bill Baroni, the only Republican to support marriage equality, and Governor Jon Corzine, who worked tirelessly to get the votes that just weren't get-able. To Senate President Richard Codey, who posted marriage equality for a vote despite the odds being against it, and to Senators Nia Gill, Sandra Cunningham and Teresa Ruiz who gave passionate speeches on the floor of the Senate — it is an honor to serve with all of you.

And last, a special thanks to the Senators, Republican and Democrat, who opposed marriage equality, but in their speeches and in press releases admitted that New Jersey's Civil Union Law was not working and did not provide the equality required under the New Jersey Constitution.

Your words helped frame the legal challenge that will!

Rev. Martin Luther King Jr. giving his "I Have A Dream" speech during the Freedom March. Washington, DC, August 28, 1963 - Photographer: Francis Miller.

Photo from the LIFE magazine photo archive.

The ultimate measure of a man is not where he stands in moments of comfort and convenience, but where he stands at times of challenge and controversy.

~Dr. Martin Luther King Jr.

table of
CONTENTS

Kim Taylor and
Deb Schlater

Lou Storey and
Stephen Theccanat

Jen and Erica
Sciolla

John and Ernie Ramos

What's L O V E got to do with it?
Everything.

It's not often we have an opportunity to change society and how we treat each other as human beings. It occurs a few times in our lifetime, if it occurs at all. We have that opportunity today. We can change fear to love, hate to compassion, cruelty to kindness.

~Senator Raymond J. Lesniak
speaking to the NJ State Senate
January 7, 2010

INTRODUCTION

Senator Raymond J. Lesniak

I recently learned Ed Sullivan threatened to "out" Jerome Robbins as a fag (Sullivan's word) if he didn't reveal members of the Communist Party to the House Committee on Un-American Activities. *Who would have thought?*

Likewise, when the New Jersey Supreme Court ruled that same sex couples had a constitutional right to the same rights and obligations as heterosexual couples, but stopped short of ruling same sex couples had a right to marry, I called Steven Goldstein, founder of Garden State Equality, to offer my congratulations. Boy did I get an ear full. "It's not enough! It's wrong! We deserve the right to marry," screamed Goldstein. *Who would have thought?*

When I shared that conversation, if you could call it a conversation, with my girlfriend, Salena Carroll, a Commissioner of the New Jersey Civil Rights Commission and a Board member of Garden State Equality, and said how off the wall Goldstein was, I got ear full number two.

That was the beginning of my transformation from a supporter of gay rights to an advocate for gay rights. I realized that recognition of same sex marriage was much more than allowing same sex couples to marry - much, much more.

> I've seen the hurt that disowning your authentic self, your true self, can do to a human being. *And I've seen the joy and the love when someone is free to embrace who they are.* I came to believe that the recognition of same sex marriage would be uplifting for our entire society.

I called Loretta Weinberg and asked if I could be her prime co-sponsor of the Marriage Equality Act. And the journey began. As the saying goes, we left everything on the field, not missing any opportunity to get a vote.

We were hoping for a miracle that never came. *What's Love Got To Do With It?* tells the story of the struggle. The final chapter is yet to be written.

Marriage Equality

top left:
Melissa Kelly and
Michiko Hilton

center:
Joey and Carrie Moran

bottom left:
Dr. Ethan Ciment and
Michael Suchman

STORIES
of tragedy, triumph and love

Jose and Jenn

JENNIFER

A message to Senator Lesniak

So, there's this man that I know...

He is 43 years old. He's always faced challenges in his life – born into poverty, always suffered from illnesses such as asthma, allergies, skin conditions, etc. He is the oldest of four children, so, no matter what, he has had to be a role model without anyone asking him. He stepped into the role of father, brother, teacher, mentor and friend for his three younger siblings. He went on to college and then business school without anyone's academic or financial help. Through my eyes, he is perfect. He is one of the most loving and generous men I have ever met. He is a great man, he is my brother. A man whom I love immensely.

> From the very bottom of my heart, thank you for fighting for his rights.

This e-mail was sent to Senator Raymond J. Lesniak after the Senate Judiciary Committee voted 7-6 to release the Marriage Equality Act for a vote by the entire Senate.

JOHN OTTO

Address to the Senate Judiciary Committee
December 7, 2009

Hello. My name is John. I'm 16 years old, a sophomore in high school, and I'm a gay male.

I first came out to my parents in middle school, and from the first realization of my sexual orientation my parents were, and continue to be, extremely supportive. I was hesitant to come out to my friends but, knowing how much they love me, I told them I was gay, and they simply responded, "Okay. That's cool."

My good friends have been there for me ever since, perhaps even more than they were before I told them about my sexual orientation. By the beginning of the 9th grade school year, I was open to everyone that I knew. But last year, when I was a freshman in high school, I became the target of bullying and harassment from other students, based solely on my sexual orientation. I had a very difficult time, as anyone would, dealing with the constant verbal abuse. It's not easy walking down the hallway, having names and derogatory terms hurled at you like you are some kind of animal being brutally stoned to death. Faggot, queer, homo – they all hurt my self-esteem and made me feel worthless. It was so hard to get myself up in the morning and walk to school, knowing very well what was to come and knowing that hardly anyone would stand up for me and my rights. And what's even worse is knowing that our state government also views me, just like those bullies in school viewed me.

> In New Jersey, I am a second-class citizen, someone who does not have equal rights, someone who it is perfectly okay to treat differently according to the state government.

Alone and depressed, and thinking about all of the things happening at school, I became extremely sad. I tried to numb the hatred, but when the numbness went away, the hatred inevitably remained. I became suicidal, and my parents got me immediate help at a residential psychiatric care program. And now I'm on the long journey back to being the funny, smart, and empathetic son that my parents had almost forgotten about.

I've endured more discrimination and hatred than anyone should ever have to deal with in a lifetime. Marriage equality is extremely important to me, because one day I do hope to get married and make a life together with one very special person, just as my two wonderful parents have done. And although many things can happen in the future, and I cannot say for sure that I will marry, I certainly do not want to have one road completely blocked from me: the road to a happy and lifelong marriage.

> I want to have the same rights that heterosexual marriage ensures, and I'm asking the members of this Senate Committee to stand up and give me that chance.

Jessie Petrow-Cohen (left) and her sister
courtesy of Garden State Equality

JESSIE PETROW-COHEN

Address to the Senate Judiciary Committee
December 7, 2009

Hi, my name is Jessie Petrow-Cohen, and I live with my moms, my sister, my three dogs, our gecko, our hermit crabs, our guinea pigs, and our snails in Maplewood, New Jersey. To me, a family is a group of people who love each other and are willing to do anything for one another.

Let me tell you a little bit about my family. Like most families, mornings are crazy, and one of us will usually leave the house without something pretty important. Between walking the dogs and making lunches, everyone is just running around, trying to get out of the door.

Wednesdays are insane. There's gymnastics and Hebrew school, and someone usually needs to go to a friend's house to pick up homework. And, of course, we have to get home in time to watch *Glee*.

We have holidays together with grandparents, cousins, aunts, and uncles, we go on vacation together. And my parents are at every sports game and competition my sister and I have ever had. I tell them everything about school and friends.

I feel that my family is no different than any of yours, except for just one thing. In New Jersey, where we live together, we are a family; but legally we are not. When anyone is curious about my family, I'm glad to tell them. When I told my friends I would be coming here today, they went home and begged their parents to come to support me. In fact, one of my closest friends, is here with us today.

The only thing that's different from my family and every one of yours is that we have to stand here and ask you if we can legally be a family, when you can be one without asking anybody. I think that us having to do something like this may just make our love for each other stronger. But it's gotten to the point where it just isn't fair. When I fill out forms in the beginning of the year, it says mother's emergency number and father's emergency number. In 4th grade, we were making Father's Day cards. And even though I don't have a father, a teacher made me write one to an imaginary one. It was crazy.

On Back to School Night, my sister had to write a letter to our parents and was required to follow a format on the board including "Dear mom and dad." It's these little things over and over again that set my family apart from being totally normal. Because other than the fact that some people don't want to give my parents the right to get married, we are.

While some of these situations are unfair, our friends and neighbors are very supportive and helpful. Last December, my house had a very serious fire, and the whole community of Maplewood was amazing. People we barely knew offered us a place to stay in their home. For two months after the fire, the doorbell rang at 6:00 every night, and a delicious, homemade dinner was brought to us. People took down our clothing sizes and went out and bought totally new wardrobes.

{ So if you're worried that the people of New Jersey aren't ready to accept us, I'm here to tell you that they have been for a while. So please, I would really like to be able to dance at my parents' wedding. }

Marsha and Louise with their son Scott
courtesy of Garden State Equality

MARSHA SHAPIRO *and*
LOUISE WALPIN

Address to the Senate Judiciary Committee
December 7, 2009

MARSHA SHAPIRO: Hello, my name is Marsha Shapiro, and this is my partner of over 20 years, Louise Walpin.

We are here today to speak and support S-1967.

LOUISE WALPIN: We brought four children into our relationship. Two, Scott and Aaron, had significant disabilities. We raised our children as one family; so much so that when Aaron, who was born with profound cognitive and physical disabilities – Marsha's biological child – turned 18, I was awarded legal guardianship by the State of New Jersey, a responsibility which I took very seriously given the fact that the disabled are often a very vulnerable population.

We were religiously married by an ordained, heterosexual rabbi 17 years ago and have a Jewish marriage license which we honor. We entered into a domestic partnership and then a civil union to obtain legal protection.

{ When looking for a job approximately one year after civil unions took effect, I found that many employers did not offer civil union benefits. }

Although I'm an advanced-practice nurse and should have many opportunities for jobs, this limited my job search as Marsha is in private practice and I maintain health coverage for the family.

In addition, at each job interview, I was forced to ask the question: Do you offer civil union benefits? That forced me to come out at every single job interview to every single prospective employer.

Did I get turned down for jobs because of my sexual orientation? I don't know. But I do know that having a separate term to identify same-sex relationships makes such job discrimination a possibility in New Jersey. This caused me a great deal of anxiety at a time when I was taking care of our children and also my dad who is dying from Alzheimer's.

I finally got a wonderful job only to learn within the past month that my place of employment is going under a self-insured model and we therefore fall under ERISA. I have been told explicitly by the administrators that the civil union benefits which I have now I will have in 2010, but they cannot guarantee that they will offer civil union benefits in 2011. So at the age of 58, will I be forced to look for a new job, or should Marsha go without health insurance coverage because insurance for a self-proprietor is so prohibitive? Neither alternative sounds palatable to me.

MS. SHAPIRO: Our children required expensive, special programs, medical equipment, and therapies to help them reach their potential. This has left us with insurmountable debt, yet this is the least of it. While Scott has grown tremendously, and we are very proud of him, he will always need our help as there is no cure for those on the autism spectrum.

To make matters worse, in July of 2008 we had to sit day after day watching our beautiful boy Aaron get sicker and sicker, experience more and more pain, until he finally went into a coma and died just three weeks before his 21st birthday and one day after my birthday. No parent should ever suffer the loss of a child.

Research indicates that 85 percent of legally married couples divorce after having only one disabled child, let alone what we've had to endure. With all this, our relationship still survived and continues to flourish. If this isn't a marriage, what is?

MS. WALPIN: It's unfair to watch your child suffer because he's different than others. It's unfair to lose a child. It was unfair that my dad who loved children so much never got to know our future daughter-in-law or the children that will come from their relationship. But none of this was within anyone's control.

> The State of New Jersey has promised us that civil unions would provide us with all the benefits of marriage, but it has failed to do so despite the fact that we have lived up to all of the obligations. This is also very unfair.

It is within your power today to right this injustice. Our family has suffered enough unfairness. I implore you, we implore you to provide us with our civil rights and legal protection that we need. Please vote for full marriage equality.

Thank you so much for your time.

Marsha and Louise among the supporters of
Marriage Equality outside the N.J. Statehouse

photo courtesy Garden State Equality

STEVEN GOLDSTEIN

Garden State Equality Chair
December 4, 2009

A deeply personal moment

It had been rumored that more than 250 Hasidim were coming to Trenton to oppose our rally and lobby day for marriage equality. About 20 of them showed up.

Most of the Hasidim there - observant members of my Jewish community who wear black hats and coats - were not rabbis, as some journalists wrote. The dress is customary for Hasidic men. Our side, in fact, had way more rabbis in support, including rabbis from Judaism's Reform, Reconstructionist and Conservative movements. They were among our more than one thousand supporters at the State House, including people of all faiths and none.

I'm going to say something that may seem hard to understand and I hope you're all not disappointed in me. Please try to understand. When I see the Hasidim protest my being gay, I am not filled with hate or even resentment. When I see Hasidim, I see people with whom I have something in common. They and I are members of *Klal Yisrael*, the Jewish community. I see my brothers and sisters. Well, that day I saw only my brothers because there were no Hasidic women there, best as I could tell.

I'm studying to be a rabbi in my other life. I cherish my Judaism deeply. In fact, every day of my life I believe I live in exile from where I should be living - in Israel - but personal circumstances would never allow me to leave my family in the United States. And that has had its blessing. I never would have met my partner Daniel otherwise.

Though the Hasidim, my fellow members of *Klal Yisrael*, disdain Daniel's and my relationship, do I still love them? I do. It is an unbreakable bond.

And so I went up to each of them, and spoke to them in depth. And I listened to things that were painful, including how I commit *toevah*, according to Leviticus - that my being gay is an abomination.

{ I cried inside. But there was one moment I cried above all others. }

One young man - he, like many of the other Hasidim, was much younger than he looked because of his beard and *payes*, his sidelocks - came up to me and asked to talk in private. So we did.

He questioned me on how it felt to be a Jew attracted to someone of the same sex and to be in a "gay marriage." I answered, "It's been a long day, I'll listen. But please, can we make this just a few minutes?"

He said, "You don't understand. I don't know how I feel about 'gay marriage.'"

I was surprised. More than surprised. I had just seen him protesting.

He continued. "I have attractions to people of the same sex. I think it's wrong but I don't think it's wrong. I know it will never go away no matter how much I try. It's who I am and I can never say that in my community."

"*Yeshayahu*," he called me (he saw my Hebrew name embroidered on the *yarmulke* I wore) "how did you get to the point in life where you could be who you are, a Jew, a gay person and in a relationship you don't have to lie about?"

{ I stopped crying inside. It all came out, tears down my face. }

Here I was with one of my brothers who bared his soul. I put my hand on his arm, in a butch way as a substitute for the embrace I wanted to give him but couldn't, because there were other Hasidim glaring at us from a distance.

And then as the rest came up to us, he read to me Leviticus, in Hebrew, on how my life was an abomination. I simply listened, and as he finished, I wished him good luck.

And he got up, joined the others, and as he walked away, he looked behind. He smiled. I smiled back.

On my ride home an hour later, I could not stop crying. I will always remember my fellow brother in *Klal Yisrael* not with resentment, but with love.

Hasidic protesters in front of the New Jersey Statehouse
photo by Tony Kurdzuk/The Star-Ledger

SALENA CARROLL

Member, N.J. Civil Rights Commission

Over the course of the marriage equality debate, many opponents have argued that society should maintain discrimination in marriage because same sex couples cannot procreate.

I want to share a story of two people I know, Gerry and Al.

They met in 1969.

They worked for the same company.

They lived in Newark, down Neck to be exact.

He was Irish; she was Italian. Neither family was happy about their courtship. Both families thought their children could each do better based solely on the nationality of the other. It was the only time their families actually agreed.

He had traveled the world for seven years with the Army and Air Force during Vietnam; she had never spent a night away from her parents.

He experienced many of the world's pleasures; she was determined to wear white at her wedding.

Despite their differences, through love letters, dates filled with dancing and other innocent romances they fell in love and married in March of 1971. And, they were ready to start their family.

> But by the end of 1975, no baby bump had appeared and they decided to tell family and friends they were looking to adopt.

In January 1976, Gerry's sister-in-law called her. She knew-a-friend-who-knew-a-friend with a pregnant teenage daughter and she thought her daughter was not ready to raise a baby. The mother of the teen wanted to place the child in a good Catholic home. Almost immediately, lawyers were contacted, social service visits were scheduled and six weeks later on February 27, 1976, Gerry picked up the phone and heard the two words that would change her life forever: Think pink. Her prayers to St. Anthony had finally been answered, she was a mother, her baby was here, her baby was healthy, and as an added bonus, it was a girl!

Three days later, Gerry and Al brought their little six pound blonde haired, blue-eyed baby girl home and named her after Gerry's parents.

Almost immediately, they learned that this was not an easy baby. She was colicky, a fever prone child and rather picky about everything. Gerry has told me on several occasions that she lost sixty pounds in the baby's first six months. This child never wanted to sleep – ever.

But Gerry and Al were great parents. She stayed home to raise this finicky, but happy, little girl and made sure all her needs were met; while Al worked hard to make sure there was always a nice roof over their heads, a great meal on the table, stylish clothes on their backs and an annual family vacation. It was a typical American family. Although unnatural some argue.

As their daughter got older, Al became much more involved than he was during those early baby years.

While their daughter grew from a baby to a toddler and eventually into a young woman, on any given weekend, you could find her and her father hitting softballs in the park, bowling, fishing, eating ice cream cones at Baskin Robbins or shooting free throws in the driveway.

The family wasn't well off, but both parents sacrificed so she could receive a good Catholic school education, pre-K through high school. And, they made sure she went to college without taking out a single loan.

When their daughter was about 18 and headed off to college, they realized their marriage had exhausted itself. After 23 years of married life, Gerry and Al knew their daughter was the only commonality they still shared and now she was out on her own.

There was a separation period and an eventual divorce. During the divorce proceeding lawyers, mediators and judges asked a lot of questions: questions about finances, questions about insurance policies, questions about alimony and questions about the responsibilities they still had to their only child, the child they raised but did not conceive.

{ During the legal process of dissolving the marriage, the judge did not ask if they naturally produced this child in order to confirm a marriage had actually occurred. Their marriage was not nullified due to their inability to procreate. }

Throughout the legal proceeding, Gerry and Al were hostile toward each other. Divorces are ugly. They forgot why they were first drawn to each other. And, for a while, it wasn't pretty.

But one day, shortly after the divorce was finalized, their little girl who was then 19 was rushed to the hospital by ambulance with extreme abdominal pain and severe dehydration. Doctors had many theories: appendicitis, ectopic pregnancy or an array of possible ruptured organs, some life threatening diagnoses. Gerry and Al were scared, and they found comfort in each other through their shared love of their daughter. They decided on that day, they would become friends once again.

Thankfully, all of the prognosis were wrong. After a lot of needles, scans and tests it was discovered that their daughter ate a bad gyro that night and the tzatziki sauce was sour. It was a simple case of extreme food poisoning. But Gerry and Al kept their promise to each other. Although they could not be a couple again, they realized they had a very special bond. No one would ever love this little girl as much as they did, and they worked on forming a partnership that first revolved around their child, but wound up developing into a deep respect for one another and an eventual close friendship.

Over the next few years, as their daughter was off discovering herself and the world around her, her parents talked several times a day. Her mom would call her and say "Call your dad". And, her dad would call her and say, "Call your mom," if she went more than a few days without her calling one or the other. They were good parents and great friends to both each other and to their little girl.

Although when I sit and really look at their daughter, I cannot believe they liked or approved of all the decisions she made in her life; but, if they didn't, you would never know by talking to either one of them. They both describe her as the smartest, prettiest, most put together woman they have ever met, they will tell you she is perfect and they both take complete ownership of how great they think she turned out.

Sadly, Al cannot brag about his baby girl to his friends anymore. He passed away on October 27, 2007 with his little girl, then a 31-year-old woman, by his side.

During the days of preparing for and attending Al's wake and funeral services, Gerry was there for her little girl every step of the way. Sometimes comforting her daughter; sometimes driving her daughter crazy. But that's what real moms from real families do with their daughters, isn't it?

I am the child of Gerry and Al. I decided to share my personal story after Assemblyman Michael Patrick Carroll (no relation) responded to Raymond's blast e-mail to all legislators seeking their support for marriage equality:

> I abide that effort with the greatest anticipa-
> tion. I look forward, especially, to the section
> on how society benefits from subsidizing non-pro-
> creative relationships, as well as to the section
> on how a constitution can be legitimately "inter-
> preted" to compel an unwilling populace to subsi-
> dize relationships which serve no public purpose.
>
> And, finally, I look forward to the section which
> demonstrates, in an intellectually and logically
> consistent matter, why the state should give a
> rat's patoot about "love".
>
> Cordially,
> mpc

In January, I chatted through Facebook and Blackberry for several days with Assemblyman Carroll on this issue. I always appreciated his honesty and I think we had fun debating back and forth with each other; I found him articulate, intelligent and most importantly accessible, honest and a very nice man. I do not want to single him out in any way as a bad guy for his opposition of such an important issue. I actually think he is a very good guy who just happens to disagree with me. And, most importantly, I truly respected his honesty throughout the entire debate.

> But when Carroll listed the overwhelming rea-
> son to deny marriage to same sex couples as
> their inability to naturally procreate, it hit a nerve.
> He basically said, if you cannot procreate, you
> cannot be a real family. It was the first time I felt
> the opposition to marriage equality personally.

Being a straight woman, marriage equality does not really affect me. I have always been a vocal supporter of all equality because I believe every American deserves to be treated the same under the law. I believe strongly in marriage equality because there are so many gay people in my life whom I truly love. I want their relationships to be protected under the law; I want them to have the same legal benefits my married straight friends enjoy; and, I want the partners of my gay loved ones to have the same legal responsibilities as the spouses of my straight loved ones.

In honesty, I never truly understood what this movement was about. To me, it was always about fairness and the legal arguments about equality.

{
It was not until I felt that MY family, MY parents and the large part of ME that is defined as daughter was questioned as real, that's when I finally got what this all means. Marriage Equality is about making families real.
}

Thank you Assemblyman Carroll.

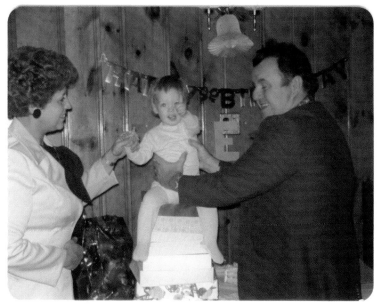

Gerry, Salena and Al

photo courtesy of Salena Carroll

EVOLUTION
of equal protection and civil rights

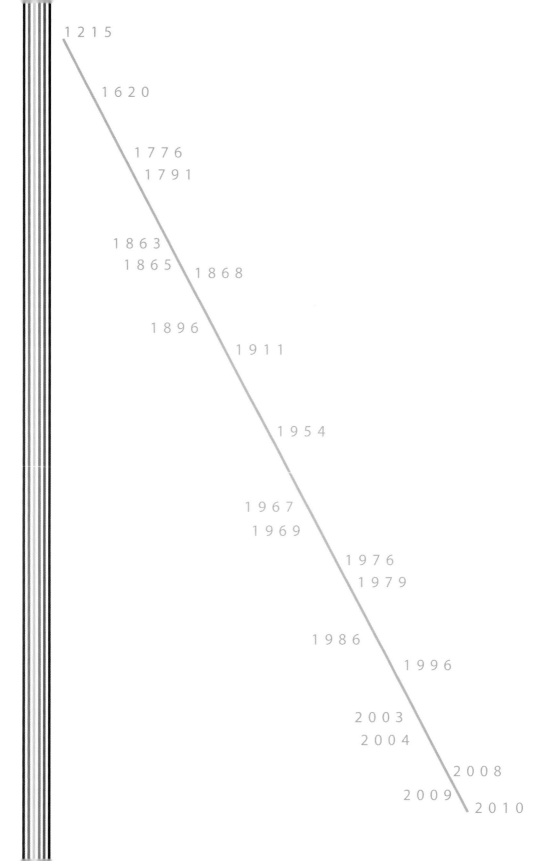

1215

1620

1776
1791

1863
1865
1868

1896

1911

1954

1967
1969

1976
1979

1986

1996

2003
2004

2008
2009
2010

1215

MAGNA CARTA

The "Great Charter of English Liberties" guaranteed certain rights of free men. This became the basis for constitutional law and influenced the development of many constitutional documents, including the U.S. Constitution.

1620

FLIGHT TO AMERICA

English citizens flee to America to escape discriminatory practices based on religious beliefs.

July 4, 1776

DECLARATION OF INDEPENDENCE

Adopted by the Second Continental Congress announcing the 13 American colonies were independent states and no longer a part of the British Empire.

September 17, 1787

UNITED STATES CONSTITUTION

Established by "We the People," the Constitution is the basis of law in the United States. It has been amended many times to continue the evolution of equal protection and civil rights.

December 15, 1791

BILL OF RIGHTS

The first 10 amendments to the Constitution are ratified by three-fourths of the states, establishing rights of the people.

January 1, 1863

EMANCIPATION PROCLAMATION

President Lincoln issues the Emancipation Proclamation, declaring "that all persons held as slaves" within the rebellious states "are, and hencefor-ward shall be, free."

December 6, 1865

THIRTEENTH AMENDMENT

Officially abolishes slavery and involuntary servitude.

July 9, 1868

FOURTEENTH AMENDMENT

"No State shall . . . deny to any person within its jurisdiction the equal protection of the laws."

February 3, 1870

FIFTEENTH AMENDMENT

The right … to vote shall not be denied … on account of race, color, or previous condition of servitude.

May 18, 1896

PLESSY V. FERGUSON

The Supreme Court of the United States upholds a Louisiana law requiring that trains provide separate but equal railroad cars for white and black passengers.

August 18, 1920

NINETEENTH AMENDMENT

Prohibits each state and the federal government from denying any citizen the right to vote because of that citizen's sex.

May 17, 1954

BROWN V. BOARD OF EDUCATION, TOPEKA, KANSAS

This landmark Supreme Court of the United States decision overturned the 1896 decision in Plessy v. Ferguson and orders the integration of America's schools with "all deliberate speed." Chief Justice Earl Warren writes that the doctrine of separate but equal has no place in education as "separate educational facilities are inherently unequal."

July 2, 1964

CIVIL RIGHTS ACT OF 1964

Outlaws racial segregation in schools, at the workplace and by facilities that served the general public.

June 7, 1965

GRISWOLD V. CONNECTICUT

The Supreme Court of the United States ruled that the Constitution protected a right to privacy. The case involved a Connecticut law that prohibited the use of contraceptives.

June 12, 1967

LOVING V. VIRGINIA

In Loving v. Virginia, the Supreme Court of the United States holds that states cannot ban interracial marriage since "the freedom to marry has long been recognized as one of the vital personal rights essential to the orderly pursuit of happiness by free men."

January 22, 1973

ROE V. WADE

The Supreme Court of the United States held that a woman's right to an abortion is determined by her current trimester of pregnancy. The Court rested these conclusions on a constitutional right to privacy emanating from the Due Process Clause of the Fourteenth Amendment, also known as substantive due process.

June 30, 1986

BOWERS V. HARDWICK

The Supreme Court of the United States ruled that Georgia's anti-sodomy laws do not violate the Fourteenth Amendment. In a concurring opinion written by Warren Burger, the Justice noted that condemnation of homosexual activity "is firmly rooted in Judeo-Christian moral and ethical standards."

May 20, 1996

ROMER V. EVANS

The Supreme Court of the United States strikes down Colorado's "Amendment 2," which forbid local governments from drafting legislation protecting gays against discrimination.

September 21, 1996

DEFENSE OF MARRIAGE ACT

The federal government defines marriage as a legal union exclusively between one man and one woman.

June 26, 2003

LAWRENCE V. TEXAS

The Supreme Court of the United States strikes down the state's "Homosexual Conduct" law. The majority opinion finds "no legitimate state interest" in these laws so directly impacting one classification of people. This decision overturns the 1986 case Bowers v. Hardwick.

November 18, 2003

GOODRIDGE V. DEPARTMENT OF PUBLIC HEALTH

The Massachusetts State Supreme Court rules that state statutes barring same sex marriage are in violation of the equal protection and due process clauses of the state constitution.

May 15, 2008

SAME SEX MARRIAGE IN CALI.

The California Supreme Court finds that laws limiting marriage to opposite-sex couples violate the state constitutional rights of same sex couples, thus granting any couple the right to marry. But in November, California voters strip same sex couples of the freedom to marry by 52 to 48 percent, amending the state constitution to define marriage as a union between one man and one woman.

October 10, 2008

KERRIGAN V. COMMISSIONER OF PUBLIC HEALTH

The Connecticut Supreme Court allows same sex couples to marry, ruling that the state's civil union law does not meet the standard of equal protection.

April 3, 2009

VARNUM V. BRIEN

The Iowa State Supreme Court rules that the state's ban on same sex marriage violates the equal protection clause of the state constitution.

April 9, 2009

SAME SEX MARRIAGE IN VERMONT

The Vermont State Legislature votes to override the governor's veto of legislation making marriage legal for gays and lesbians.

May 6, 2009

SAME SEX MARRIAGE IN MAINE

John Baldacci became the first governor in the nation to sign a same sex marriage bill. Maine voters overturned the law on November 3, 2009 by 52.8 to 47.2 percent.

June 3, 2009

SAME SEX MARRIAGE IN N.H.

Legislation for same sex marriage was signed into law making New Hampshire the fifth state to legalize same sex marriage.

December 18, 2009

SAME SEX MARRIAGE IN D.C.

Mayor Adrian Fenty signs a bill passed by the Council of the District of Columbia. The District became the only jurisdiction in the United States below the Mason–Dixon Line to allow same sex couples to marry.

NEW JERSEY'S EVOLUTION

January 12, 2004
DOMESTIC PARTNERSHIP ACT
The "Domestic Partnership Act" created a "mechanism ... for New Jersey to recognize and support the many adult individuals in this State who share an important personal, emotional and committed relationship with another adult."

October 25, 2006
LEWIS V. HARRIS
The New Jersey State Supreme Court unanimously found that "unequal dispensation of rights and benefits to committed same sex partners can no longer be tolerated under our State Constitution."

December 21, 2006
THE CIVIL UNION ACT
In response to the Lewis v. Harris holding, the Civil Union Act revised New Jersey's marriage laws and created civil unions. The bill aimed to grant same sex couples the same rights and privileges as married couples.

December 10, 2008
CIVIL UNION REVIEW COMMISSION
The Civil Union Review Commission unanimously reported that civil unions did not grant equal protection to same sex couples. The Commission recommended that New Jersey revise its marriage laws to be gender neutral and thereby institute marriage equality.

January 7, 2010
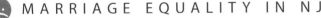
MARRIAGE EQUALITY IN NJ
New Jersey Senate votes 20 to 14 against the Marriage Equality Act.

March 18, 2010
NJ LAWSUIT FILED
Motion filed in New Jersey Supreme Court to grant same sex couples the right to marry.

SUPPORT

for marriage equality

featuring
JULIAN BOND

NJ CLERGY MEMBERS

CHILDREN AND ADULTS
FROM AROUND THE STATE

JULIAN BOND
Civil Rights Leader

Speech to the Senate Judiciary Committee
December 7, 2009

Mr. Chairman, members of the Committee, thank you for allowing me to testify before you in support of Senate Bill 1967, the Freedom of Religion and Equality in Civil Marriage Act.

I actually don't live in Georgia anymore, but live in the nation's capital. I'm proud to say that last week our city council voted 11-2 to legalize same sex marriage, and I'm here to urge you to do the same. That's because I believe gay rights are civil rights. As my late neighbor and friend Coretta Scott King said in 1998, "Homophobia is like racism and anti-Semitism, and other forms of bigotry, in that it seeks to dehumanize a large group of people, to deny their humanity, their dignity, and their personhood." That is why – although the NAACP has no position on same sex marriage – in 2005 the NAACP Board of Directors unanimously passed a resolution stating: "The NAACP shall pursue all legal and constitutional means to support non-discriminatory policies and practices against persons based on race, gender, sexual orientation, nationality, or cultural background."

We acted in order to ensure equal protection under the law for all, and to create a more civil and just society. Black people, of all people, should not oppose equality, and that is what gay marriage represents. It does not matter the rationale: religious, cultural, pseudo-scientific; no people of good will should oppose marriage equality. And they should not think that civil unions are a substitute.

{ At best, civil unions are separate but equal, and we all know *separate is never equal.* }

Two years ago we celebrated the 40th anniversary of a case aptly called Loving v. Virginia, which struck down anti-miscegenation laws, and many years later allowed my wife and me to marry in the state that declares "Virginia is For Lovers." Then, as now, proponents of marriage as is, wanted to amend the United States Constitution. Introducing a constitutional amendment in 1911 to ban interracial marriage, Representative Seaborn Roddenbery of my former home state of Georgia, argued; "Intermarriage between whites and blacks is repulsive, and adverse to every sentiment of pure American spirit. It is abhorrent and repugnant. It is subversive to social peace. It is destructive of moral supremacy." Does any of this sound familiar? Then, as now, proponents of marriage as is invoke God's plan. The trial judge who sentenced the Lovings said that when God created the races he placed them on separate continents. The fact that He separated the races showed that He did not intend for the races to mix. Well, God seems to have made room in his plan for interracial marriage. He or She will no doubt do the same for same sex marriage. No less an expert on the subject than Mildred Loving understood, herself, this. Widowed many years ago, she chose to live a very private life, turning down countless requests to be interviewed, to make appearances, and to be honored. But on the 40th anniversary of this ruling, three members of Faith in America visited her, seeking her support for gay marriage. She was undecided, and remained so for several days. When she eventually agreed to allow her name to be used in support of gay marriage, she was asked, "Are you sure you understand? You're putting your name behind the idea that two men, or two women, should have the right to marry each other." Mildred Loving replied, "I understand it, and I believe it."

That's when I'm asked, "Are gay rights civil rights?" My answer is always, "Of course they are." Civil rights are positive, legal prerogatives; the right to equal treatment before the law. These are rights shared by everyone. There's no one in the United States who does not, or should not, share in enjoying these rights.

> Gay and lesbian rights are not special rights in any way. It isn't special to be free from discrimination. It is an ordinary, universal entitlement of citizenship.

The right not to be discriminated against is a common-place claim we all expect to enjoy under our laws, and our founding document, the Constitution. That many had to struggle to gain those rights does make them precious, but it does not make them special, and it does not reserve them only for me or restrict them from others. And they should never be subject to popular votes. When others gain these rights, my rights are not diminished in any way. My rights are not diluted when my neighbor enjoys protection from discrimination. He or she becomes my ally in defending the rights we all share.

For some people, comparisons between the African-American Civil Rights Movement and the movement for gay and lesbian rights seems to diminish the long, black historical struggle with all its suffering, sacrifices, and endless toil. However, people of color ought to be flattered that our movement has provided so much inspiration for others, that it's been so widely imitated; that our tactics, our methods, our heroes, our heroines, even our songs, have served as models for others. No parallel between movements is exact. African-Americans are the only Americans who were enslaved for more than two centuries, and people of color carried the badge of who we are on our faces. But we are far from the only people suffering discrimination; sadly, so do many others. They deserve the law's protections and civil rights too. Sexual disposition parallels race. I was born black, and had no choice. I could not, and would not, change it if I could. Like race, our sexuality isn't a preference. It is immutable, unchangeable, and the Constitution protects us all against discrimination based on immutable differences.

{ Many gays and lesbians worked side by side with me in the Civil Rights Movement, and many do so now. Am I to now tell them, "Thanks for risking life and limb, helping me win my rights," but they're excluded because of a condition of their birth? They can't now share in the victories they helped me to win? That having accepted and embraced them as partners in a common struggle, I can now turn my back on them and deny them the rights they helped me win, that I enjoy because of them? Not a chance. }

We know there are many whose opposition to same sex marriage is religiously based; but they ought not force their beliefs on people of different faiths, or people of no faith at all. In addition to being a civil right, marriage is a civil rite – that's R-I-T-E. If you don't want gay people to marry in your church, all right. But you shouldn't say they can't be married in City Hall because of your religious belief. Black Christians have always discarded scriptures that damned us in the name of religion, like the curse of Ham in Genesis or support for slavery in Ephesians. We should just as easily and just as eagerly discard those which marginalize others.

For 20 years I sat where you sit now, as a member first of the Georgia House, and then the Georgia Senate. There were times when popular sentiment and my constituents said, "Vote this way." And I said no, because I thought this way was the wrong way. Although I can't claim to have always done it, I always felt better when I acted on conscience, instead of following the popular choice.

I close where I began by asking you to cast an affirmative vote when this legislation comes before you. You'll be standing for right, and on the right side of history.

Thank you, Mr. Chairman, members of the Committee, for giving me this time.

photo by Richard Avadon

CLERGY

Monday, January 4, 2010
Senate President Richard J. Codey
Assembly Speaker Joseph J. Roberts, Jr.
The State House
Trenton, New Jersey 08625

Dear Senator Codey and Speaker Roberts:

We are 120 clergy members across New Jersey from 19 faiths and denominations. We are but a sample of New Jersey clergy who support marriage equality and wish to marry same sex couples legally.

We are Baptist, Buddhist, Episcopal, Ethical Culture Society, Interfaith, Jewish Conservative, Jewish Reconstructionist, Jewish Reform, Lutheran, Metropolitan Community Church, Methodist, Presbyterian, Reformed Church of America, Sankey Tribe, St. Francis of Assisi Catholic Church, Unitarian Universalist, United Church of Christ and Unity Fellowship Church. Among us are members of the Religious Society of Friends, the Quakers, who do not have clergy.

We 120 clergy members ask you to put the marriage equality bill to a vote in your respective houses - without precondition - before the end of the current legislative session.

In our nation founded on the separation of church and state, the State of New Jersey should not be in the business of telling faiths and clergy whom we can or cannot legally marry. We take issue with the State's current marriage law, which is not religiously neutral but reflects the beliefs of leaders of a particular faith community which opposes marriage equality.

We 120 clergy members support the freedom of religion embodied by the U.S. Constitution, the New Jersey Constitution and the marriage equality bill now before the New Jersey legislature, the Freedom of Religion and Equality in Civil Marriage Act. Language in the bill underscores the right of every religion and every clergy member to decide whom to marry and not to marry.

Furthermore, an amendment to the bill passed by the Senate Judiciary Committee last month would codify the nation's strongest protections for religious freedom in matters of marriage. The amendment ensures that no religious organization or religious facility in New Jersey can be sued because it has followed its conscience in which marriages it chooses to accommodate, or not accommodate.

There cannot be a better guarantor of religious freedom than the version of the Freedom of Religion and Equality in Civil Marriage Act now before you.

We are proud that our nation has never allowed any one religious doctrine to determine secular law. New Jersey law provides for divorce, for example, though some find divorce religiously impermissible. Indeed, the idea of New Jersey's banning civil divorce would be unthinkable. Our state would not stand for favoring the convictions of any one religion over another.

As 120 clergy across New Jersey from 19 faiths and denominations, we urgently ask you to put the marriage equality bill to a vote in your respective houses - without precondition - before the end of the current legislative session. The State must get out of our sanctuaries and uphold our religious freedom as clergy to marry whom we wish, or don't wish, under state law.

We appreciate your thoughtful consideration.

Sincerely,

Rabbi Joel Abraham, Jewish Reform

Rabbi Victor Appell, Jewish Reform

Rev. Meg Barnhouse, Unitarian Universalist

Bishop Mark Beckwith, Episcopal

Leader Rafaela Billini, Buddhist

Rev. Fred Blanken, Sankey Tribe

Rev. David C. Bocock, United Church of Christ

Rev. Dr. Thomas Bohache, Metropolitan Community Church

Rabbi Neal Borovitz, Jewish Reform

Rabbi Andrew Bossov, Jewish Reform

Rabbi Kenneth L. Brickman, Jewish Reform

Rev. Christopher Bruesehoff, Lutheran

Rev. Rene Colson Hudson, American Baptist

Dr. Joseph C. Chuman, Ethical Culture Society

Rev. Matthew Cimorelli, Lutheran

Rev. Diana Clark, Episcopal

Rev. Susan Nelson-Colaneri, Lutheran

Rabbi Faith Joy Dantowitz, Jewish Reform

Rev. Bruce Davidson, Lutheran

Michael Dawson, Religious Society of Friends (the Quakers)

Rev. Peter DeFranco, Lutheran

Rev. David DeSmith, Episcopal

Rabbi Stephanie Dickstein, Jewish Conservative

Rev. Robert Janis-Dillon, Unitarian Universalist

Rev. Thomas Dorsey, Lutheran

Rev. Wayne Dreyman, Lutheran

Rev. L.L. DuBreuil, United Church of Christ

Rev. Dr. Jeffrey C. Eaton, Lutheran

Rev. Rusty Eidmann-Hicks, United Church of Christ

Rabbi Paula Feldstein, Jewish Reform

Rev. Mary Forrell, Lutheran

Rev. Bryan Franzen, Presbyterian

Rabbi Elyse Frishman, Jewish Reform

Rev. Maristella Freiberg, Episcopal

Rev. Anahi Galante, Interfaith

Rev. Debra Given, Presbyterian

Rev. John Graf, Interfaith

Cantor Meredith Greenberg, Jewish Conservative

Rabbi Jarah Greenfield, Jewish Reconstructionist

Rabbi David Greenstein, Jewish Conservative

Rev. Carol Haag, Unitarian Universalist

Rabbi Debra R. Hachen, Jewish Reform

Rev. Dr. Betsey Hall, Presbyterian

Rabbi Richard Hammerman, Jewish Conservative

Rev. Rose Hardy, Liberation in Truth Unity Fellowship Church

Rev. Rose Hassan, Episcopal

Father Joseph A. Harmon, Episcopal

Rev. Margaret Hayes, Lutheran

Rev. Alicia Heath-Toby, Liberation in Truth Unity Fellowship Church

Rev. Margaret Herz-Lane, Lutheran

Bishop Jacquelyn Holland, Unity Fellowship Church

Rev. Janyce Jackson, Liberation in Truth Unity Fellowship Church

Rev. Seth Kaper-Dale, Reformed Church in America

Catherine Karsten, Religious Society of Friends (the Quakers)

Rev. Katherine G. Killebrew, Presbyterian

Rabbi Donna Kirschbaum, Jewish Reconstructionist

Rev. Robert Kriesat, Lutheran

Teacher Peter Kurczynski, Buddhist

Rabbi Alfred Landsberg, Jewish Reform

Rev. Gary C. LeCroy, Lutheran

Rabbi Darby Jared Leigh, Jewish Reconstructionist

Rev. Fred Lentz, Lutheran

Rabbi Ellen Lewis, Jewish Reform

Rabbi David C. Levy, Jewish Reform

Rabbi Adina Lewittes, Jewish Conservative

Cantor Erica J. Lippitz, Jewish Conservative

Rabbi Sharon Litwin, Jewish Reform

Bishop George Lucey, St. Francis of Assisi Catholic Church

Rev. Murdoch MacPherson, Lutheran

Rabbi Randall Mark, Jewish Conservative

Rev. Alison B. Miller, Unitarian Universalist

Rabbi Jordan Millstein, Jewish Reform

Rev. Manish Mishra, Unitarian Universalist

Rev. Rob Morris, Presbyterian

Rabbi Leana Moritt, Jewish Renewal

Rev. William C. Moser, Lutheran

Rabbi Robin Nafshi, Jewish Reform

Rev. Julie Newhall, Unitarian Universalist

Rev. Tiina Nummela, Lutheran

Rev. Clark Olson-Smith, Lutheran

Rev. Sara Olson-Smith, Lutheran

Rev. Charles Bluestein Ortman, Unitarian Universalist

Rev. Michelle Owings-Christian, Sankey Tribe

Rev. Fairbairn Powers, Episcopal

Rev. Dr. Susan Veronica Rak, Unitarian Universalist

Rev. Ann Ralosky, United Church of Christ

Rev. Donald R. Ransom, Unity Fellowship Church

Rabbi Esther Reed, Jewish Conservative

Rev. Christine Regan, Episcopal

Rev. Elsie Rhodes, Presbyterian

Rabbi Jonathan Roos, Jewish Reform

Rabbi Francine Roston, Jewish Conservative

Rev. Dr. Charles T. Rush, United Church of Christ

Rev. Leah Doberne-Schor, Jewish Reform

Rev. Marshall Shelly, Episcopal

Rabbi Rebecca Sirbu, Jewish Conservative

Rabbi Steven Sirbu, Jewish Reform

Rev. Carlton Elliott Smith, Unitarian Universalist

Rev. Vanessa Southern, Unitarian Universalist

Cantor Kerith Spencer-Shapiro, Jewish Reform

Rabbi Cy Stanway, Reform Judaism

Rev. Randy Steinman, Lutheran

Rev. Charles Stephens, Unitarian Universalist

Rev. Douglas Stivison, United Church of Christ

Rev. David L. Stoner, Lutheran

Thomas Swain, Religious Society of Friends (the Quakers)

Rebecca Sylvan, Religious Society of Friends (the Quakers)

Elder Rev. Kevin E. Taylor, Unity Fellowship Church

Rabbi Elliott Tepperman, Jewish Reconstructionist

Rev. Matt A. Thiringer, Lutheran

Rev. Charles N. Thompson, Presbyterian

Rev. Mary Tiebout, United Church of Christ

Rev. Ray VandeGiessen, Presbyterian

Rev. Gus Vinajeras, Lutheran

Rev. Paul Walker, Episcopal

Rev. Moacir Weirich, United Church of Christ

Rev. Dr. Traci C. West, United Methodist

Rev. David Wolf, Episcopal

Rev. Jeffrey B. Ziegler, Lutheran

Rabbi Ruth A. Zlotnick, Jewish Reform

CHILDREN

Dear
I wont my parre to get maried dond
my preart are tomoms my mom
told me thatwe need marriage
equality before they can get
married

Please pass marriage equality

joemi
age 9

Hi, I'm a 10 year old who has two moms.
Some may think I'm weird or different,
but at my house it's no different than
my best friend who has a mom and
dad. The one thing I don't get is
WHY are we different? WHY Can't
my parents get Married? I strongly
suggest you change the law and let my
parents get married. This law will make
happier people and a brighter future.
Please CHANGE the law!!!
Sincerely,
Ally

Hi, I'm Zan and I 9.
I support marriage equality.
My family has love
even though I have 2
moms, I think a man and a
man and a woman and a woman
should have the right
to marry. Pleas consiter
my eguile even though
I'm hot 18, Thank
you for your time,
Zan

49

A D U L T S

Dear Senator,

I am a lifelong resident of New Jersey. I urge you to vote in support of the Marriage Equality bill this Thursday. On Valentine's Day of 2007, I asked my long-term partner Brian for his hand in "marriage" three days before civil unions became legal. We wed in September of that year. While we consider ourselves married, the rest of the world sees only the quotation marks. You have the power to right that wrong.

When New Jersey passed its civil unions law in 2006, New Jersey residents thought it would finally mean equality for our state's gay and lesbian couples. But three years later, we have learned that only marriage can protect the rights of New Jersey's families.

That's why I'm writing you today. I want to urge you to support legislation guaranteeing the right of gay and lesbian couples to marry, before it's too late.

We're not yet certain of all of Governor-elect Chris Christie's positions, but we're sure of one thing: He will not support marriage for gay couples. Governor Corzine has just two weeks to sign marriage into law, which he swore to do. Your vote for equal rights has never mattered more.

A state commission found last year that gay and lesbian families suffer because civil unions are not equal to marriages. same sex couples routinely face discrimination in health care, taxes, education, and virtually every aspect of their lives because people are confused by the meaning of the alien term "civil union."

> Civil unions establish the rights of gay couples on paper, but they deny gay couples those rights in practice.

Marriage equality would also do more than protect the rights of gay and lesbian couples – it would boost the finances of an economically battered New Jersey. People would flock to our state for weddings, while others would choose to move to New Jersey, knowing they can live their lives in the security only a marriage can provide.

I sincerely hope that I can count on your support for this piece of legislation, so important to my partner and me and the State of New Jersey's reputation for taking a stand for individual rights.

Respectfully,

Douglas

Dear New Jersey Senators,

I know the bill for marriage equality is coming up for a vote on Thursday and I would like to urge you all to vote yes. I deeply want my family and many friends to be allowed the same rights that I am allowed.

This is not a "gay issue," it is a human rights issue.

Thank you for your time.

Sincerely,
Jenna

Please vote "YES" for full marriage equality. Civil Unions don't work and hurt NJ families. If Mexico City can get it right, don't tell me New Jersey is going to get it wrong.

Best Regards,
Megan

As a 55 year old lesbian, a life-long registered Democrat, first domestic-partnered with my "spouse" in 2004 and then civil-unioned with her in 2007 (with my dear partner for over 20 years now, been through a lot, including her brain tumor surgery), I want you to realize separate is not equal.

This is not a religious issue; it is a civil rights issue, an economics issue, a healthcare issue.

I expect Democrats to make sure this important issue is voted on!

Susan

I am writing this in the hopes that your most conservative colleagues would please try to understand the lives of gay persons – especially the lives of religious gay persons.

As was shown yesterday with clergy raising their SUPPORT for marriage equality, there is a growing number of welcoming churches and indeed many churches and synagogues now welcome gay parishioners who are in monogamous relationships but actually bless such unions from the United Church of Christ, Episcopal Church, Evangelical Lutheran Church, Reform Judaism, Conservative Judaism, MCC, Unitarian, Methodist, etc.

Indeed country after country throughout the world is moving towards MARRIAGE equality – e.g., Canada, Sweden, Netherlands, Norway, Belgium, Spain, South Africa. Cities and states throughout the world are moving towards it as well – with the latest being Mexico City. Make no mistake that history is moving towards acceptance despite the opposition of a very vocal and powerful extremist fringe...

Please treat gay couples equally. There can be no doubt that relegating gay persons to what some call 'sham' relationships that are not marriage is not equal and is nothing short of government-endorsed inequality.

Please, I urge you to urge your colleagues to talk to gay couples and especially gay Christians before choosing to vote against the marriage equality. For what it's worth, thanks for listening. God bless.

Luke

SPEECHES
on Marriage Equality

Featuring Senators

LORETTA WEINBERG

RICHARD J. CODEY

RAYMOND J. LESNIAK

BILL BARONI

NIA H. GILL

M. TERESA RUIZ

SANDRA B. CUNNINGHAM

JOHN A. GIRGENTI

SEAN T. KEAN

GERALD CARDINALE

senator L O R E T T A   W E I N B E R G

Senate Voting Session
January 7, 2010

For almost 40 years, I was privileged to share a life with my husband. I never had to explain or justify our relationship to anyone. It was our relationship built on trust, love, compassion, humor, and a great deal of understanding.

My partner happened to be a man, so our relationship was legally entitled to be called marriage. But men and women do not have a monopoly on loving relationships. Men and women, or man and woman, don't have exclusive rights to relationships built on trust, love, compassion, and everything else that bonds two people together.

We all know same sex couples who enjoy the same love, and trust, and compassion that are shared between a man and a woman, between a husband and wife. Who are any of us, that we have some special knowledge that let's us deny marriage, as inappropriate, to loving and committed same sex couples. Same sex couples are entitled to the same legal protections, the same societal acceptance, and the same ability to honor and celebrate their love, as is everyone else.

For those who somehow fear the undoing of society by allowing same sex marriage, we're kidding ourselves. A vote against same sex marriage is not going to end the love and commitment that is shared by same sex couples. These commitments exist, and they will continue to exist, regardless of what happens today and regardless of whatever fears and prejudices exist in the world.

> In that sense, a vote to deny equality of the law to same sex marriage is no different than any other of the controversial but ultimately correct civil rights votes in our history.

I have traveled all over this state and can tell you from my own experience, the average New Jerseyan doesn't care about anyone else's marriage. They have their own problems to worry about. The people of this state have a proud history of respect for the private lives of their neighbors. The people I've talked to and met on various campaign trails, do you know what they're worried about? Whether they're going to have a job next month, how they're going to make tuition payments, the health of their family, and the cost of their taxes. I think the average New Jerseyan is probably more worked up about the failure of the Giants to make the playoffs than whether same sex couples can get married.

Political calculations are unspoken but always the present issue lurking at the edge of every major decision that we make here today. I know people are concerned about primaries from political fallout. But remember, not a single legislator from New York, Massachusetts, Vermont, Connecticut, or California who voted for civil marriage since 2004 ever lost their bid for re-election. Not one.

There are few times in this body that we are truly called upon to act on our conscience. To me, today is one of those days. This is not just another roll call vote. The vote goes to the heart of who we are as a body, a state, and ultimately as individuals. Today we have the ability to recognize the love and commitment that is shared by same sex couples. Unfortunately, we read so much in the news about broken families and broken homes. Yet we deny people who love each other the right to officially share their lives as married couples. It doesn't make sense.

To my colleagues who are wavering, do what your conscience tells you to do. Vote yes. Those of you who are pulled by religious principles must understand that this bill will not compel any religion or any clergy member to do anything that they wish not to do. And thanks to Senator Baroni's amendments, this has been completely clarified.

But we should also acknowledge that there are large groups of clergy, including the rabbi of my own synagogue, who want the ability to legalize such marriages within their congregations.

And before I close, I'd like to first single out one person and one entity. This has been a long struggle, and I suspect it's a struggle that is going to have to continue. We are at this point because of the efforts of one individual and one organization: Steven Goldstein and Garden State Equality. The thousands of people who have come out to show their support in Trenton and across this state have put a needed face on this issue. The mothers, the fathers, grandparents, and, indeed, children themselves who live within these loving family units – whether gay, straight, in a partnership, or simply aspiring to one – the members of Garden State Equality and all of these people, in their own dignified way, have reminded us all why this is so important. To them, I thank them for helping us get this far.

{ And I make them this promise: Their day will come; whether it is today, their day will come, I know. }

I'm not a lawyer, but let me close with a quote from the dissenting opinion in the Supreme Court's shameful separate but equal decision in Plessy v. Ferguson. And the quote is: "In view of the Constitution, in the eye of the law, there is, in this country, no superior, dominant, ruling class of citizens. There is no case here in respect of civil rights. All citizens are equal before the law."

And I close – here is another quote, this one from Henry David Thoreau in Walden. And that goes:

"It is never too late to give up your prejudices."

I want to particularly thank my co-prime sponsor Ray Lesniak. This has been a long road. I think we are both looking forward to this day with much anticipation, and to the days that come when the State of New Jersey will recognize marriage for same sex, committed, loving couples.

Thank you very much.

senator R I C H A R D J . C O D E Y

Senate Voting Session
January 7, 2010

Let's be honest, in the last month or so our offices have been very busy. Most times it's hard to get through to your legislative office because we've been lobbied. Whether it's one side or the other, whether it's the groups or just individuals, they have lobbied us and lobbied us extensively. That's their right. That's democracy at its best. We've been elected to make these decisions, like the decision that we will make today.

So why are we here today, at this moment in time? To me, it's one word, strong word, marriage. That is why we're here today. It's just that one word and nothing else. And what it really boils down to for me is the other word, equality.

{ Whether it's the right to vote, to get on a bus, to use a water fountain, to get a job, exchange legal wedding vows – all of those rights many of us today take for granted. And maybe it's because we didn't have to fight for those rights. }

When the Declaration of Independence was signed, there was this understanding of equal. Let me repeat what equal was in terms of the right to vote then. They said you had to be white, you had to be male, you had to be Protestant, you had to be over the age of 21, and you had to have owned land. At that time, that was equality and that was accepted. Now, looking back, we all ask ourselves, what were these great men thinking? What were they afraid of?

Then later on in our country's history, we had a Civil War. Six hundred thousand Americans lost their lives before that War ended, all over the issue of slavery. All of us, when we look back on that time in our nation's history, we have to ask ourselves, what were they thinking? What were they afraid of?

And then, years later, another movement started in this country called the Suffrage Movement, to give females the right to vote in this country. Can you imagine that in our nation's history that women and some men had to protest, had to march, so that women in this country had the right to vote? It's so hard to imagine that that movement took 70 years before females in this country had the right to vote in 1920. It's unbelievable. So again, looking back, you have to say to yourself, what were they thinking? What were they afraid of?

You know, my grandfather used to show us pictures of immigrants getting off the boat in New York. And he would show us pictures of the employment companies – the large companies in our state – that had employment offices in the cities. And there were signs in those offices that said, "Irish need not apply, Jewish need not apply;" later on, "Italians need not apply." And do you know what? Nobody raised the issue of Civil Rights. At that point in time it was an acceptable practice in this country. Looking back, we have to ask ourselves, what were they thinking? What were they afraid of?

Back in 1967, there were 26 states in this country – not New Jersey – that banned interracial marriage. Today you would say, what was wrong? What were they thinking? What were they afraid of that they had to ban interracial marriage?

You know, just a few decades ago in this Legislature we debated and we passed bills giving females in the workplace equal pay for equal work. It took so long to get those rights. Again I would say to you, what were they thinking? What were they afraid of?

I can remember, as a young teenager, one year my dad got enough money and took myself and my brothers to Florida for a couple of days. And he took us to a ball game. And we saw something that startled us. And what we saw was bathrooms for whites and bathrooms for blacks, fountains for whites and fountains for blacks. It was something we read about. But seeing it in person, we were incredulous. And that's basically all we talked about – what we saw in Florida that night. And it stayed with us forever. I mean, think about that. That was legal back in the '60s. I mean, what could those people have possibly been thinking? And what were they afraid of, to do that?

Sometimes in our lifetime, issues like this have been brought before the Supreme Court: Brown v. Robertson. I could go on, and on, and on. But let me, for a moment, say this: Let us assume today the bill passes, it passes the Assembly, it gets signed into law. What in our lives, regardless of your sexual orientation, is going to change? Where are you going? What do you have to be frightened about if this were to become law? How does it change anybody's daily life? The lives of your spouses, your children, people at work? I don't know. Is it going to affect our children at school? I don't think so. I don't understand it. So I don't understand the rationalization of why some people are so strongly against this particular bill.

And by the way, just anecdotally, how many times have you heard some-one say to you, "You know, there was a gay couple who moved on our block?" And you know what, nobody ran outside to put a for sale sign up, nobody bought more locks for their house. They found out that people with a different sexual orientation were just like them. They were good neighbors, they were good citizens, they were nice people to talk to. And it didn't change their lives in any way, shape or form.

Again, what is it that we have to fear today that's contained in this bill? Okay, their sexual orientation may be different. But so what? What does that mean? What change does it bring about?

So I hope that sometime in the not so distant future, a senator in this chamber, would have to get up and say, "You know, in 2010 they were debating the issue of whether or not people of the same sex should get married," and have him or her say, "What were they thinking back then? What were they afraid of?"

{ So are we so certain at this point in time that we have finally reached the limits of acceptance and compassion for our fellow citizens? Let us do the right thing today. Let's not make any more of our citizens wait to enjoy the benefits we all do. }

In thinking back, I have to say to myself that, when I entered the legisla-ture 36 years ago almost today, that I would not be voting on a bill for domestic partnerships, that we would not be voting for a bill for civil unions or for gay marriage. And I think back then that was accepted rationale. But this is 2010, and the time is now. There is nothing to be afraid of; nothing at all.

Thank you all very much. I appreciate that.

senator R A Y M O N D   J .   L E S N I A K

Senate Voting Session
January 7, 2010

I'm wearing my American flag tie today. I was inspired to wear it by Senator Bateman, who wore his American flag tie when the Senate Judiciary Committee took testimony on the Marriage Equality Act. He wore it in memory of Pearl Harbor Day and the Americans who fought and died for our liberties and our civil rights. I commend Senator Bateman for recognizing and honoring our veterans.

I believe Senators Dougherty, Girgenti, Haines, Rice, Singer, and I are the only New Jersey Senators who have served in our military.

> We served alongside, knowingly and unknowingly, gay soldiers who put their lives on the line to protect our liberties and civil rights.

We served alongside American heroes who had to hide and deny their sexuality in order to fight for the freedoms and liberties we enjoy today.

During the Civil War, World Wars I and II, and the Korean War, African-American soldiers laid their lives on the line for our liberties and civil rights. Before General Eisenhower ended segregation in the military, they had to endure the indignity of being denied equal status with their fellow soldiers. Those who were fortunate to come back to America had to endure the indignity of being treated as second- and third-class citizens and, in some cases, noncitizens.

I don't have standing to make the argument that marriage equality and gay rights are both civil rights. Senator Gill gave the most eloquent and compelling speech in the Judiciary Committee on the civil rights issue and, no doubt, will be equally eloquent and compelling today. I will rely on her arguments and, indeed, Senate President Codey's arguments, and the words of Julian Bond. In his testimony before the Senate Judiciary Committee, this icon of the Civil Rights Movement said, "Many gays and lesbians worked side by side with me in the 1960s Civil Rights Movement. Am I now to tell them, 'Thanks for risking life and limb helping me win my rights,' but they're excluded because of a condition of their birth, that they can't share now in the victories that helped me to win they helped me to win? That having accepted and embraced them as partners in the common struggle I can now turn my back on them, deny them the rights they helped me win, the rights I enjoy because of them? Not a chance. No." Julian Bond.

Senator Cardinale has proposed to put marriage equality on the ballot, just as the New Jersey Legislature did in 1914 when the voters rejected women's right to vote by a 58 to 42 percent margin. Thankfully, six years later, the New Jersey Senate voted 18 to 2 to ratify an amendment to the United States Constitution giving women the right to vote. Now Senator Allen, Senator Beck, Senator Buono, Senator Cunningham, Senator Redd, Senator Ruiz, Senator Turner, and Senator Weinberg honorably serve in this august body.

We've received 120 letters from clergy of 19 different religious denominations supporting marriage equality. The Unitarian Church in Somerset Hills, the Living Waters Lutheran Church in Flemington, the Unitarian Church in Washington Crossing, the Unitarian Church in Princeton; the Unitarian Church in Montclair, the Emmanuel Lutheran Church in New Brunswick, the St. Paul Lutheran Church in Teaneck, the Grace Lutheran Church in Camden, the Ridge of Peace Community Church in Camden, the B'nai Keshet Synagogue in Montclair, St. Stephens Episcopal Church in Millburn, Trinity Episcopal Church in Asbury Park, Faith United Church of Christ in Union, First Congressional Church of Christ in Montclair, and String of Pearl Synagogue in Princeton – all want the right to practice their religious beliefs and perform same sex marriage, but our law prevents them. We discriminate against them and, by that discrimination, endorse some religions over other religions. Government has no business endorsing one religion over another.

This great country was founded by patriots who fled from England where government endorsed one religion over another. Their passion for individual freedom was so strong they left their homeland to come to America in the hope that a government in a land of the free and the home of the brave would not interfere with their religious beliefs.

Unless we vote for marriage equality, we will be interfering with the religious beliefs of many of our citizens. Government is wrong to interfere with religious beliefs. Today we can right that wrong. Unless we vote for marriage equality, we will be violating Article I, Section 3 of the New Jersey State Constitution, which states, "No person shall be deprived of the inestimable privilege of worshipping Almighty God in a manner agreeable to the dictates of his own conscience." In Section 4 it states, "There shall be no establishment of one religious sect in preference to another." In Section 5 it states, "No person shall be denied the enjoyment of any civil right because of religious principles." It is wrong for any government to deny any person the privilege of worshipping Almighty God in a manner agreeable to the dictates of his conscience, or to any person any civil right because of religious principles. Today we can right those wrongs by voting for marriage equality.

In the Judiciary Committee we heard the most heart-wrenching human stories of pain and suffering inflicted by our current Civil Unions law. Loved ones have been denied access to hospital rooms, denied the right to make burial arrangements, turned down for health and pension benefits because of our separate but unequal Civil Union law.

A young girl, embarrassed and confused because she couldn't say her parents were married; a young boy who contemplated suicide because he was held to be abnormal because he was gay.

These social injustices will not go away overnight if we pass marriage equality, but they will go away. If we don't pass marriage equality, they'll continue to cause unnecessary pain and suffering until we do.

This week I received the following e-mail message from Assemblyman Michael Carroll regarding the book I am collaborating on with Senator Weinberg. The book is entitled *What's Love Got to Do With It?: The Case for Same Sex Marriage*. I quote Assemblyman Carroll, "I look forward to the section which demonstrates in an intellectually and logically consistent manner why the State should give a rat's patootie about love."

Here is my answer to Assemblyman Carroll about why we should give a rat's patootie about love, and why I believe you should vote for marriage equality. It's summed up in the following passage from the Bible in the First Letter of John, Chapter 3, verses 18, 23, and 24: "My dear friends, let us love one another, because love is from God. Everyone who loves is a child of God and knows God. Whoever does not love does not know God, because God is love."

I do believe as elected officials we need to think long and hard about the lack of love in our deliberations, in our beliefs, and in our relationships with each other.

What's love got to do with it? Everything.

It's not often we have an opportunity to change society and how we treat each other as human beings. It occurs a few times in our lifetime, if it occurs at all. We have that opportunity today. We can change fear to love, hate to compassion, cruelty to kindness.

Those who oppose gay marriage are not unloving, hateful, or cruel. But our law, which does not allow for gay marriage, causes unequal and oftentimes painful treatment of loving, same sex couples. Marriage equality will take away that unequal treatment and make us more compassionate, understanding, and loving.

> I pray every day to be a compassionate, understanding, and loving human being. Some days I do not achieve those goals in my actions or in my deeds. Today will not be one of those days. Today I have an opportunity to be compassionate, to be understanding, and to be loving by my yes vote for marriage equality.

But today is not about me. It's about the rights of same sex couples from whom we've heard heart-wrenching stories of pain inflicted unknowingly and knowingly as a result of our law which fails to secure for them the rights of marriage. To guarantee these couples those rights and to relieve them of the fear and pain from being denied those rights, I urge you to vote yes for marriage equality.

After the Senate Judiciary Committee released Marriage Equality for a floor vote, I received the following e-mail. "So there's this man I know. He is 43 years old. He has always faced challenges in his life. Born into poverty, always suffered from illnesses such as asthma, allergies, and skin conditions. He is the oldest of four children, so no matter what, he has had to be a role model without anyone asking him. He has stepped into the role of father, brother, teacher, mentor, and friend for his three younger siblings. He went on to college and then business school without anyone's academic or financial help. Through my eyes he is perfect. He is one of the most loving and generous men I have ever met. He is a great man. He is my brother, a man that I love immensely from the bottom of my heart. Thank you for fighting for his rights."

Please vote yes for marriage equality.

image courtesy of The Bergen Record

senator BILL BARONI

Senate Judiciary Committee
December 7, 2009

Thank you, Mr. Chairman. I thank you.

First of all, Mr. Chairman, as we began the debate about marriage, I quoted yourself, saying that it's going to be a fair, open, and professional day. And Mr. Chairman, there is no doubt, for anyone who has sat through the last eight hours or whatever we're up to now, that you have run a profoundly fair, open, and professional hearing. Everyone in this room, regardless of their opinion on this matter, has had the opportunity to have their vision heard. You have provided exceptional leadership today. I am grateful for it, and I must say that our loss next year will certainly be the Budget Committee's gain, as you will bring that skill to them. And Mr. Chairman, thank you.

So today, this was a question about balance. In my opening remarks I talked about balance. And this was a tough debate. We heard from folks on all sides of this issue: we've heard from folks who have deeply held religious beliefs on all sides of this issue. We have heard from people who believe the Civil Union law has not worked for them, or anyone else. We have heard from religious leaders who want to be able to have gay marriage. And we've heard from a whole lot of kids who look at all of us up here and go, "What's the big deal?"

To me, this has always been about balance – balancing the right of religious institutions, organizations, and societies to practice their religion, free from government. Protect them, those religions that choose not to – those organizations, those groups that choose not to recognize gay marriage. Today we have passed the most profound, far-reaching religious protection amendment anywhere in the country, by this Legislature.

The other balance I spoke of was the right of all New Jerseyans to be treated equally, and we heard hundreds of those stories. Stories of New Jerseyans who just want their relationships, their love, to be treated the same as everybody else's. They wanted government to stay out of their relationships. Equality. Equal treatment at law. That is not too much to ask.

{ And I am fully understanding that tonight, right now, I will be the first-ever New Jersey Legislator in this state, on the question of marriage equality, to say the following: I vote yes. }

senator N I A   H .   G I L L

Senate Voting Session
January 7, 2010

I would just like to reference the fact that you don't have to go back a thousand years to talk about marriage being defined as a man and a woman, and that that has always been the definition; because it hasn't. You could go back to 1967, *Loving v. Virginia*; and they said that a black woman or black man and a white woman or white man could not marry, because the concept of marriage – handed down through generations – never contemplated that white and black people would marry, or that there would be interracial marriage.

{
So that the definition of marriage has been delineated by color and by race. And the court found that to be a violation of the equal protection clause. And that is exactly what is happening now.
}

And why does it matter? It's because we have already taken State action. We are debating this issue as if we have not committed to a course of action. The Civil Union law says, and I quote: "The Legislature has chosen to establish civil unions by amending the current marriage statute to include couples (*sic*). In doing so, the Legislature is continuing a long-standing history of inequity (*sic*) by providing same-sex couples with the same rights and benefits as heterosexuals."

So we inched into amending. And when I questioned the representatives of the Catholic Church, they said that they support civil unions. So we're not here talking about an issue of morality. They said they support it, and I questioned the gentleman. They supported civil unions because it gave to same-sex couples all the rights and benefits of heterosexual married couples. And that is the basis upon which, so he represented, that the Catholic Church supports civil unions.

And when I questioned: if civil union does not provide the same rights and benefits, what should we do? And in that questioning, he simply kept returning to the fact that civil unions, in fact, provide the same rights and benefits as a heterosexual.

So the issue of a cultural change recognized by this Legislature – that cultural change was already recognized and sanctioned in domestic partnerships. That is where the sea change happened.

And so we have taken State action. And that State action – much like they did in Virginia in defining who could marry – that State action, once it creates an unequal situation, it violates the Constitution. So I don't think, humbly, that we are here debating in a vacuum. We have to look at what State action have we taken as a Legislative body. That State action says the intent of civil unions is to give all benefits and privileges that heterosexual married couples have.

And then they go on to enumerate. And one important one for me, among others, was the issue of insurance. And we know – as was testified at the judiciary – there's an Oxford Insurance plan – national corporation – and you know how they define dependents or spouse? And I quote, "Spouse:" – this is a benefit update rider – "A person's partner, husband or wife in a legal marriage. For purposes of dependent eligibility under this certification, spouse includes same-sex partners who are married in jurisdictions that recognize same-sex marriage."

There is nothing you can do to tweak this Civil Union law to address the issue that same-sex couples are denied the benefits of insurance under national insurance companies, because we have a separate and unequal system.

Now you could have, respectfully, as many task forces as you want. But you cannot change the fact that national companies are defining dependency for insurance – health insurance – benefits as same-sex couples who are married. And so when you look to see what State action have we taken, and does that State action provide all the benefits and rights as a heterosexual married couple – and the answer is a resounding no.

And so we have, I think, an obligation under the Constitution legislatively, because we have taken this State action. And Martin Luther King talks about, and I quote, "Sometimes a law is just on its face, and unjust in its application." "For instance," he goes on, "I have been arrested on a charge of parading without a permit. Now, there's nothing wrong in having an ordinance which requires a person to have a permit for a parade. But such an ordinance becomes unjust when it is used to maintain segregation and to deny citizens their constitutional rights."

{ So on its face, our Civil Union law may appear just; but it is, in its application, based on what we said as a Legislature that we wanted to happen in civil unions, that it becomes unjust and in violation of the equal protection clause. }

Is this a civil rights issue? Well, is the right for disabled people to have reasonable accommodations and the ability to fully participate in this society? That's a civil rights issue. Is the right for our children, if they have a disability, to be part of the full educational process in this country? That's a civil right. Is it a civil right when they say if you are charged – even in a civil case – you have a right to know what you are being charged with? That's a civil right. And so the civil right issue is so fundamental because of the 13th and the 14th amendments, but particularly the right of equal protection. And each of us, in some way, in this chamber has a family member – if not ourselves – who has benefited from others taking an issue and standing up for civil rights in some way when it was not popular. And it wasn't popular when we wanted to do certain things with our children, when we wanted to take issues and make people full-fledged citizens of this country. And it wasn't until 1965 that African-Americans in parts of this country even had the right to vote.

So once you take this State action, as a legislative body you can't just – I would submit – back away and talk about what would have been done; because it has already been done. And so if we look to the original intent of the Constitution, before Reconstruction women did not have the right to vote. And there's not a woman in here, I submit, as a Legislator or as a member of our staff in any capacity, who would have been here today unless legislators around the country took a position that we will fight – for a what? A civil right. And so just because this is not a racial injustice, it does not mean that it's not a civil right injustice.

And Martin Luther King also said that he was cognizant of the interrelatedness of all communities and states. We know that he said, "Injustice anywhere is a threat to justice everywhere. We are caught," he said, "in an inescapable network of mutuality tied in a single garment of destiny. Whatever directly affects one, affects all of us." We may not even like our gay-partner neighbors. And you know what? We have the right to. They may even argue with each other, and you know what? They have the right to. But this body cannot abdicate its responsibility once we have taken State action. That State action must be constitutional in its equal protection.

And before I close, how do we fix the issue of denying people health insurance benefits – so that if you have the Oxford plan, but you are a same-sex civil union in New Jersey, one of you could be covered and the other could be on charity care? Living under the same roof, raising children, living in a loving relationship, but you cannot be covered under the insurance. So one partner stands in line for charity care, and the other has insurance. This strikes so fundamentally at what is important to us.

And I would like to say that I understand that this would be a difficult vote. But there's never been a civil rights vote that's been easy. Because in granting another person their civil rights, we must reach past our level of personal comfort. And I must commend not only the sponsors, but Senator Baroni, because they have carved out and said, "If you don't believe in civil marriage in your religion, don't do it." And you know what? The State's not going to force you. And not only do you not have to do it in your church, you don't have to do it in any affiliate, or in any hall, or any club that's affiliated with you. The strongest First Amendment protection in this nation.

And so, one: it gives that protection. Two: the Catholic Church said the only reason they supported civil unions is, it did what? It gave all the same benefits as heterosexual couples. And we see that is not true. And lastly, of all: This chamber, this Legislature, would not be this diverse and this encompassing of the citizens of the United States if someone had not said to my forefathers and mothers that we will fight for the right for our children to be equal participants in this society. And I know that the same-sex couples here, they're not just fighting for themselves; they're fighting for their children. They're fighting for their future. They're fighting to be able to say to their children what my grandfather and grandmother were able to say to their children: "We won the fight. You can vote. You can go to school. You can make out of your life that what you think is important. But we have fought so that you could be a full participant in America."

> Let these same-sex couples be a full participant
> in our State. Thank you.

photo courtesy of Trevor Powell

senator M . T E R E S A   R U I Z

Senate Voting Session
January 7, 2010

I'm not an attorney, so I won't cite court cases. I don't have prepared remarks, but as I sat back and I listened to everyone's testimony, it became clearer and clearer why it is so important to vote yes today.

When Governor Codey took us through episodes of history, I placed myself in that given moment, and I will tell you in every incident I would have been considered "the other."

> When Senator Lesniak said if it were not for great changes, individuals like myself would not be included in this great arena of the State House to serve on the behalf of people, I knew how critically important it was.

When Senator Baroni talked about a space where only certain individuals were allowed to come in, I knew that I did not want to be the other person on the other side. See, because for too long an individual like myself has always been told, "You can't. You don't look like. You shouldn't be. Perhaps not now, maybe later."

If I have the opportunity to continue to serve here, and the honor and privilege, I don't ever want to take a vote that says, "It's okay for me, but not for you."

senator SANDRA B. CUNNINGHAM

Senate Voting Session
January 7, 2010

Because I have been taught all of my life what it means to stand up for what we believe in, and to fight for our rights. I use slavery, because many of us think of slavery as so far away, and people say, "Why are they still talking about slavery?" Well, it's really not that far away for many of us. My father-in-law's father was a slave. He was an 8-year-old boy who probably would have been the child who fanned the white slave masters and their guests at dinnertime. And I can remember my husband telling me that he grew up hearing from his father that he was told that as a little boy his grandfather went to church and always heard how God wanted us to be in slavery. He always recited scriptures, because they always talked from scriptures about how blacks were not equal – they were unnatural. They needed to be taken care of and God put the white masters there to protect them.

And this little boy grew up teaching his children and his grandchildren the importance of being a human being – of fighting for your rights. As an African-American, I cannot in good conscience not support anyone's right to fight to be treated with dignity and respect. I wonder how any of us, as lawmakers, can even contemplate not supporting everyone's right to have the kind of life that we all want to have. Whether you personally agree with it or not, you have a right, as a lawmaker, to stand and to support the people in this state. And all of us are not all alike. But all of us have a right to dignity, we have a right to love, we have a right to respect. And we, as lawmakers, need to ensure that that's what we're doing. If it was not for the Civil Rights Movement, the African-Americans or the minorities in this room might still be here – Senator Gill said that we wouldn't be here – we would be, but we would probably be sweeping the floors instead of sitting as legislators.

So I'm asking you to put aside what you might personally feel that you would not do, but think about this: our responsibility here is to protect the rights of our citizens. And we all need to stand up and not judge, but stand up and support anyone who fights for their rights. Because they have a right to the kind of life that they want. That is the American dream.

"I've known my state Senator, John Girgenti, since he first ran for office. When I was a little girl, my mother changed political parties to help out on his campaign. We live in the same small town and our paths have crossed often. I expected to hear from him after I wrote him a very personal letter in which I told him about my cousin Beth. After Beth's partner died, Beth was denied the rights of a widow because they weren't married. Beth was overcome with grief, but society did not validate the depth of her relationship or recognize her as a widow. Instead, she was told to get over it. Without the emotional support every other widow receives, Beth succumbed to despondency and took her own life. I thought John would have responded, especially because we know each other. But he never did. **When I testified before the Judiciary committee about my family's loss, he had nothing to say. Nothing, that is, until his 'No' vote on marriage equality in the New Jersey Senate on January 7, 2010."**

-Heidi Ehman
Hawthorne, N.J.

senator J O H N   A .   G I R G E N T I

Senate Voting Session
January 7, 2010

To my colleagues, to everyone involved – this has been a very contentious issue, very spirited issue, and there have been strong feelings on all sides.

I believe that every couple in this state, same sex and opposite sex, deserve the same rights and privileges. Because of that belief, I strongly supported Domestic Partnerships and Civil Union legislation in the past. However, this bill does more than that – it changes the fundamental definition of marriage in this state. This change strikes at the heart of our society and how we define who we are. It is much bigger and more complex than just passing a law. It is a major cultural change that needs to be digested by the public.

This is what I hear from my constituents, and not just those concerned about the religious aspects, but from young, old, clergy, non-clergy, married, and unmarried. If same sex unions are not recognized, they should be by hospitals or other entities in this state; we need to fix that.

The federal government defines marriage as a union between a man and a woman; so even if this bill becomes law, benefits like certain pensions, insurance, and Social Security will still not be available to the same sex couples. And in the meantime, we have altered what most people hold most dear. I believe that we, as state legislators, have an obligation to the institution of marriage and to the traditional values that it represents. In today's world, it seems that nothing is sacred anymore. There is a lack of civility, a breakdown in nearly every institution and trust in our government, and the way of life is much reduced.

The proponents of this bill revered the terminology of the word marriage. They respect the word as much for itself, as what it may mean in practical terms; so do opposite-sex couples. They believe in the sacredness of their union – as passed down throughout the generations – to be a union of a man and a woman. I have never been a strong supporter of initiative and referendum, but in this instance I support the use of a non-binding referendum to allow the public to weigh in on this critical change in our society. If a societal reform of this scope and magnitude is ever to be passed, I believe that the voters should make their wishes clear. Some choose to chastise this position and debunk it. I disagree. Over the years, I've been a strong advocate on a number of worthwhile and sensible progressive measures. But by supporting this measure, I would not only be violating my own conscience, but in my opinion, the public conscience as well.

Because of these reasons, I will vote no on this bill.

SOME OF MY BEST FRIENDS ARE...

senator S E A N T. K E A N

Senate Voting Session
January 7, 2010

Listening very carefully to the discussion here from my colleagues – very compelling arguments made on both sides of this debate. I can tell you I have to take my hat off to the dedicated lobbyists who are up in the gallery – the folks who have been at my law office on a regular basis: Steve Goldstein and his supporters who have done a fantastic job; passionate, enthusiastic advocates for this cause.

I take difference with some of my colleagues. I believe that we are elected here to make decisions such as this, in this body. We don't need to put it on the ballot. I believe that we are elected to make these tough decisions. That's what I believe we're going to be doing here this afternoon.

I can tell you in my brief tenure in the State Legislature – six or seven years now, which I've been very proud to serve in – this is the toughest issue. I have to tell you the reason that it's the toughest issue is not necessarily because it's going to impact on the most people the most. Because I believe the gay population is probably a minority, in some respects. And we talk about financial issues, we talk about educational issues, we talk about business issues – things that cut across the entire population and impact on people a great deal. This particular issue, though, impacts on a minority perhaps more than any other issue. It's a very important issue.

Governor Codey made a great observation when he talked about the gay community. And when gay people move into the community, do the property values go down and the neighborhood turn to garbage? Well, no, just the opposite happens, in fact. When you drive around my district in Monmouth County, to places like Asbury Park and Ocean Grove, and you see the rainbow flags, just the opposite happens The neighborhood is gentrified – they push the drug dealers out. Businesses thrive; real estate values go up; the economy, in general, improves; certainly society improves. And I can tell you, I've seen that firsthand. Somebody told me today I have the gayest district in the State – the 11th Legislative District, the 25 towns in the 11th have a huge gay population. I know there's a gay population in Ocean Grove and Asbury Park, and certainly in all the other towns in my district; as well as the districts that all of you represent. But it doesn't matter where they reside. The fact of the matter is they deserve to have rights. They deserve to have things that the rest of us as Americans have. They turn neighborhoods around, as I've said. They turn struggling neighborhoods into neighborhoods where people want to live. Neighborhoods that were previously places people didn't want to go, the gay community moves in and turns it around and they share many of the same values that all of us share.

I also listened today – in fact, when I was sworn into this House, I celebrated that evening with a ceremony at a restaurant in Ocean Grove.

> Friends of mine who are gay own the restaurant and I was very proud to have my reception there and my ceremony there.

However, I hear some words being thrown about here today, words like, "What are we afraid of?" Words like "prejudice." Words like "primary elections." Well, I take offense to those characterizations of people who may not agree with the proponents of this bill. And people may ask me, "Well Kean, why didn't you support this bill today?" Throughout this process I have committed to the advocates of this bill and to the opponents of this bill – by the way, in my legislative district I've seen it's about 50-50, by the way – and I've committed to those individuals that I would keep an open mind throughout this whole process, and I have done that. I wish this was an issue where I could have just awakened one morning and said, "You know what? I know what I'm going to do; I'm either for it or I'm against it." And that wasn't the case. This issue is that important and that difficult that I kept an open mind throughout this entire process, right up to the end.

But, guess what, folks? And guess what – to those proponents of this bill that I am unfortunately going to disagree with here today – sometimes people just disagree with you. Maybe they don't share your perspective, maybe they don't share your values. Maybe they just disagree with you. Maybe I'm wrong. Maybe in disagreeing with you in some future Legislature, people will be able to come back and point out to my mistake, and my value judgments and my decisions were wrong. But I can tell you at the end of the day – I think I speak for everybody – when you lay down at night and go to sleep, you do a heart check. And that's really where you get the courage to make decisions like the decision we're going to make here today.

So what did I base my decision on? Some people characterized some of us who are opponents of this bill as just like blind sheep following some kind of a religious doctrine. I take offense to that, too. But is religion a part of that decision-making process? Of course religion is a part of that. Spirituality is part of that; life experience, education, culture, family, all of those things come into those decision-making processes. And so for you on the other side of this debate to characterize those who aren't supporting this bill as being afraid of political primaries, we're prejudiced, we're being afraid of being wrong, that's just unacceptable to me. And I think it denigrates those who are on the other side of this debate.

I'm going to be voting no. Thank you, Senate President.

photo by Frank Galipo/Special to the Press #67109

"GAYS ARE NOT NORMAL."

Sen. Gerald Cardinale from New Jersey Capital Report with Steve Adubato and Rafael Pi Roman.
Aired February 13, 2010

senator GERALD CARDINALE

Senate Voting Session
January 7, 2010

Like many of my colleagues who have spoken before me, and like all of the members of the Judiciary Committee, I sat through the hearing; I heard the witnesses. I come away with a different opinion. I heard nothing that cannot be fixed about the problems that were presented to us by folks who are in a civil union relationship. There are many problems, but for each of those problems there is a solution if we put our minds to it. And there is a solution without doing violence to marriage.

You know, there's an old saying – I hate to foster the image that I don't respect lawyers, because I do respect lawyers. But there is an old saying that has been told to me by lawyers: You put four lawyers in a room and ask a question, and you may get as many as 13 answers – 13 different opinions.

And our society functions because we don't function that way. We don't take a bunch of lawyers and put them together and ask what their solutions to a problem are. We have a process. And that process involves a Judiciary. And we have a Supreme Court, which is the top element of that Judiciary. And this question was submitted to that Supreme Court. And that Supreme Court said you can fix this inequality in one of several ways. And this Legislature met and selected a way to resolve that problem. I didn't vote for that bill – I thought it had some deficiencies. I still think it has some deficiencies. And I believe that those deficiencies can be remedied.

I have great respect for the sincerity and especially for the persistence of the sponsors of this legislation – the supporters of this legislation. But there are many who believe that this bill will change our entire culture. In my view, so momentous a change should be – must be – submitted to the people for a public vote. Now, my view is not without precedent and it is not an isolated notion. In over 30 states in this country inhabited by human beings, some of whom are gay and some of whom are straight, they have dealt with this problem. They have put it on the ballot. And in every state where it has been put on the ballot, the voters have voted to maintain marriage as between one man and one woman. I find it very difficult to believe that in all 30 of those states there is no respect for civil rights. I believe many of those states are leaders in promoting civil rights for all of their people.

Let me go on to say, I very strongly believe that the people of New Jersey are not second-class citizens. Like these others states, New Jerseyans should be trusted with self determination when momentous, cultural changes are proposed and are decided. But there are some who disagree.

There are interest groups who do not believe in trusting the people with decisions that may end up not to their liking. Some of those interest groups are very quick to suggest that we put things on the ballot if they believe it will go their way. They're not so quick when they believe that the determination may come out on another side of the question.

There may even be a few who actually prefer elitist solutions. Hey, let's recognize the fact: Every one of us in this room – whatever we consider ourselves – a lot of folks who are outside of this room think of us as elitists because we have been elected – and there are 40 of us – and there are 8 million people in New Jersey. Should we be making this decision on this cultural change? For many years we've had an opportunity to put this question on the ballot. We have not done so. But in a sense – in a very real sense – last November it was on the ballot. We had two folks who ran for governor; each of them took one side of this question. The fellow who was elected took the side of marriage between one man and one woman.

You know, I've heard that we are supporting a particular religion – and we're excluding other religions – by maintaining marriage between one man and one woman. You know, I had an opportunity maybe 10 or 15 years ago to be sitting in the diplomatic setting where a gal who sat next to me was the third wife – not consecutive – but the third current wife of a fellow who belongs to a religion where they are presumed to be allowed to have four wives. Are we going to accommodate that particular religious belief? Where does it end? I believe it should end where it has ended for 2,000 years – more than 2,000 years; thousands of years – in our society where marriage is one man and one woman.

> I respect the vote of the people this past November, and I would hope we all do, and vote against this measure.

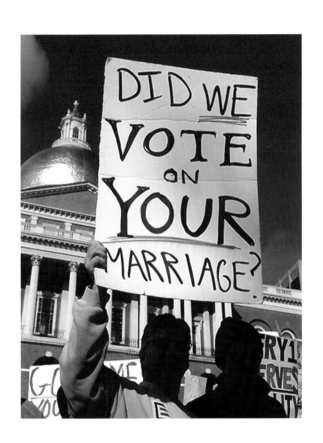

*The Senate gallery just before the final vote, a nay,
was cast to defeat the gay marriage bill, 20 to 14.
Supporters vowed a battle in State Supreme Court.*

THE VOTE

I pray every day to be a compassionate, understanding, and loving human being. Some days I do not achieve those goals in my actions or in my deeds. Today will not be one of those days. Today I have an opportunity to be compassionate, to be understanding, and to be loving by my yes vote for marriage equality.

~Senator Raymond J. Lesniak

Today we have the ability to recognize the love and commitment that is shared by same sex couples.

~Senator Loretta Weinberg

S-1967 FREEDOM OF RELIGION IN CIVIL MARRIAGE

Commonly known as the Marriage Equality Act

yea

BARONI, Bill
BUONO, Barbara
CODEY, Richard J.
CUNNINGHAM, Sandra B.
GILL, Nia H.
GORDON, Robert M.
LESNIAK, Raymond J.
RUIZ, M. Teresa
SCUTARI, Nicholas P.
SMITH, Bob
STACK, Brian P.
VITALE, Joseph F.
WEINBERG, Loretta
WHELAN, Jim

nay

BATEMAN, Christopher
BECK, Jennifer
BUCCO, Anthony R.
CARDINALE, Gerald
CONNORS, Christopher J.
DOHERTY, Michael J.
GIRGENTI, John A.
HAINES, Philip E.
KEAN, Sean T.
KEAN, Thomas H., JR.
KYRILLOS, Joseph M., JR.
MADDEN, Fred H., JR.
O'TOOLE, Kevin J.
OROHO, Steven V.
PENNACCHIO, Joseph
RICE, Ronald L.
SACCO, Nicholas J.
SINGER, Robert W.
TURNER, Shirley K.
VAN DREW, Jeff

abstain

BEACH, James
SWEENEY, Stephen M.
SARLO, Paul A.

Senator Diane B. ALLEN *was absent due to illness*
Senator Andrew R. CIESLA *was absent*

Daniel Gross, left, and his husband Steven Goldstein
of Garden State Equality after the Senate vote

photo by John O'Boyle/The Star-Ledger

"The bill fails.
Close the board."

Senate President Richard J. Codey

SUPREME COURT
of
NEW JERSEY

*Top row, l to r: Justice Roberto A. Rivera-Soto; Justice Barry T. Albin;
Justice John E. Wallace, Jr.; Justice Helen E. Hoens;
Front row, l to r: Justice Virginia Long; Chief Justice Stuart Rabner;
Justice Jaynee LaVecchia.*

E P I L O G U E

"the final chapter is yet to be written"

SUPREME COURT

of

NEW JERSEY

Docket No. 58,389

LEWIS V. HARRIS

BRIEF IN SUPPORT OF PLAINTIFFS' MOTION IN AID OF LITIGANTS' RIGHTS

March 18, 2010

Their day will come... their day will come, I know.

We absolutely had to have a vote. A benchmark needed to be set. And history needed a scorecard. We did absolutely everything we could, from field, to messaging, to process.

Everyone should know that the New Jersey effort is one of a series of steps. We will look back with pride on what we did; others will look back in great unanswerable regret.

~Senator Loretta Weinberg

ABOUT THE AUTHORS

senator
RAYMOND J. LESNIAK

Taking on a less than politically popular issue of social justice like Marriage Equality is nothing new for Senator Lesniak. He sponsored the repeal of the death penalty, making New Jersey the first state in the nation, since the U.S. Supreme Court ruled it is not cruel and unusual punishment in 1978, to recognize that "no good comes from the death penalty." The "no good" quote is from Senator Lesniak's speech at Le Memorial de Caen, Normandy, France where he became, in 2009, only the second American to win this prestigious international human rights award in the 20 year history of the competition.

Senator Lesniak is the author of *The Road to Abolition: How New Jersey Abolished The Death Penalty* and started The Road to Justice and Peace, a non-profit organization devoted to promoting social justice causes.

Serving in the New Jersey Legislature since 1978, Senator Lesniak has sponsored the most far reaching environmental protection laws in the nation.

From *Humanitarian of the Year* to *Legislator of the Year*, Senator Lesniak has been honored by a diversity of groups including the Jewish National Fund, American Cancer Society, and the Medical Society of New Jersey. In 2003, he received the *Phillip M. Scanlan Environmental Award* for his contributions to improving the environment. In 2009, he was honored by the New Jersey Business and Industry Association, the New Jersey Food Council, and the Chemistry Council of New Jersey for his legislation to revitalize New Jersey's economy. Senator Lesniak is the recipient of the *Fathers of our Children* award from the Marion P. Thomas Charter School for his efforts to improve educational opportunities for children from low income families; and was honored by The Bridge to Recovery for championing alternatives to incarceration and substance abuse treatment programs.

Senator Lesniak was N.J. Democratic State Chairman 1992-1993 and chaired the state campaigns for Clinton-Gore and Gore-Lieberman.

senator
LORETTA WEINBERG

Throughout her almost three decades as a public official, Senator Loretta Weinberg has been recognized for her strong advocacy for women, children, families, and health care. She served as a member of the Teaneck Township Council; was elected to the New Jersey Assembly in 1992; and then to the Senate in 2005.

As a member of the Assembly, Ms. Weinberg was the sponsor of the New Jersey law guaranteeing new moms and their babies 48 hours of hospital care which became the national model later signed into law by President Bill Clinton. Senator Weinberg also authored legislation promoting handgun safety; keeping drunk drivers off the roads; improving services for children with autism; and adults with aphasia. She was a prime sponsor of the landmark law to ban indoor smoking in New Jersey. Senator Weinberg is also known for her sponsorship of laws to improve ethics and transparency in government.

Loretta Weinberg graduated from the University of California with a bachelor of arts degree in history and political science. She went on to do graduate work in public administration at Fairleigh Dickinson University. She shared a loving marriage with Irwin Weinberg for 39 years until his death from cancer in 1999. Together, they ran a small business, and raised two children, Daniel and Francine, in their hometown of Teaneck. She now enjoys two wonderful grandchildren, Shayna and Jonah, along with her work in the legislature.

Senator Weinberg sponsored the first Domestic Partnership law in New Jersey; then went to work on the Civil Union legislation; and was the prime sponsor of New Jersey's Marriage Equality bill. She now chairs the Senate Health, Human Services and Senior Services Committee. She also serves on the Judiciary Committee, the New Jersey Israel Commission and the Historical Commission.

Senator Loretta Weinberg has been given numerous honors including the National Council of Jewish Women Hannah G. Solomon award; Legislator of the Year by the New Jersey Social Workers, the Jewish War Veterans, the Women's Political Caucus Barbara Boggs Sigmund award; and is honored by Garden State Equality naming a yearly recipient of the *Loretta Weinberg Lifetime Achievement Award.*

WHAT'S
LOVE
GOT TO DO WITH IT?

Loretta and Irwin Weinberg

Salena Carroll and Raymond Lesniak

EVERYTHING.